Contents

Introduction

The presentation of a war memorial is integral to its values. War memorials hold significant values for the community and there is usually a desire for them to look at their best. Although aesthetics are important, war memorials are historical monuments and ensuring their longevity through appropriate maintenance and repair is crucial. Cleaning forms part of this ongoing care: it may be considered as part of a maintenance plan for a war memorial or of more extensive repair works. Regardless, it should not be undertaken simply to restore the war memorial to an 'as new' or pristine condition, as the methods needed to achieve it are likely to be damaging. The war memorial should look cared for.

Figure 1
Algae and lichen obscure inscriptions, particularly if they are very similar in colour to the substrate beneath. Higher plants can become established in open joints.

Definition

War Memorials Trust defines a war memorial as 'any physical object created, erected or installed to commemorate those involved in or affected by a conflict or war.'

Although a war memorial might usually be thought of as a plaque, a freestanding cross or perhaps a bronze statues of a soldier on a pedestal, this definition allows for a vast array of different types.

The full range of memorials in the United Kingdom can be seen at War Memorials Online as well as researched through the Imperial War Museum's War Memorials Register.

It is not possible within the scope of this guidance to cover all the different types of memorials, so the focus is on those that are the most commonly seen across the country. These include plaques, crosses, obelisks, cenotaphs, sculpture, arches and lych-gates. Complete buildings, such as chapels, hospitals and community halls, along with objects such as windows, organs, rolls of honour, flags and seats have been excluded. However, some of the approaches covered in this guidance are still relevant; advice on the care of individual artefacts or historic fabric can be found through the Conservation Register (see Where to Get Advice).

Before considering whether to clean a war memorial, it is essential to gather as much background information about it so an informed decision about cleaning (and any other conservation works) can be made. This should not only include researching its history but also understanding the extent, nature and significance of its surroundings and being aware of any restrictions or legislation which apply to it. Each memorial is unique in its construction, location, environment and state of deterioration. It is essential to investigate the materials it is constructed from and to assess and evaluate its present condition. This information should be recorded so that it provides a basis for subsequent inspections.

Once the condition and significance of a war memorial is understood, a considered judgement can be made about the amount of cleaning (and any other conservation or repair that may be needed). Once the nature of the works has been identified, best practice includes commissioning them through a tender process and selecting a contractor with the necessary skills to carry them out to a high standard.

Many aspects of the repair and maintenance of war memorials, especially those involving complex structures, require professional involvement. Architects or surveyors are needed to inspect larger or more sensitive structures. All such professionals should be conservation-accredited by their professional body. Specialist conservators should be engaged to evaluate the condition of the materials, and carry out and supervise complex treatments. Excellent practical skills and thorough knowledge of the materials are essential to carry out repairs to the required standard, so craftspeople and conservators with suitable experience should always be used.

Volunteers are important in maintaining continuity of local involvement in the war memorials and are invaluable in any fundraising. They can also carry out much of the research and help with regular monitoring and the production and updating of condition surveys. Members of the local community also have a crucial role to play in tackling some routine maintenance work, such as pruning invasive vegetation.

Successful projects are based on a collaborative approach between professionals, craftspeople and custodian. Details of where to contact suitable professional are given in Where to Get Advice.

Further details on these aspects can be found in *The Conservation, Repair and Management of War Memorials.*

Getting consent for cleaning

Many war memorials are included in the *National Heritage List for England*. Listing celebrates buildings and monuments of special architectural or historic interest and encourages sympathetic and sustainable management. Regardless of whether listed at Grade I, Grade II*or Grade II a memorial is legally protected and any proposed work, including cleaning may require Listed Building Consent from the local authority. If it is a Scheduled Monument, or within a scheduled area, contact Historic England. Listed Building Consent helps ensure that any proposed changes maintain the monument's significance and that appropriate methods and materials are used in any repairs.

Principles of practical conservation

Conservation of a memorial should never be thought of solely in terms of practical treatment. It is intrinsically linked with the values that we associate with it; establishing these values will affect the degree of intervention that is considered appropriate. Since the mid-19th century a number of manifestos and charters have sought to set down the underlying principles that should govern the work to historic buildings and monuments. These are described in detail in *Practical Building Conservation: Conservation Basics* (2012).

A number of phrases such as 'reversibility' and 'minimum intervention' are often used to summarise these principles. However, these do not do justice to the complex series of questions that need to be asked when considering the need for intervention on war memorials.

When considering options for practical repair, there are a number of overriding criteria that should be taken into account:

- Only materials which have been demonstrated to be appropriate to the original fabric should be considered. These will normally be the same or similar to the host material. Where this is no longer possible (for example original stone is not available), the technical and aesthetic properties must be compatible with the original

- Any method should aim to be the least interventive to achieve the desired aims; this might mean using a gentle water-based cleaning system rather than an abrasive method

- Interventions should aim to maximise the life expectancy of the memorial while retaining as much of the original fabric as possible. For a memorial, this might mean deciding to retain features if they can be repaired or if they are still performing their function

- Interventions should aim for reversibility (that is they can be removed without having affected the original fabric) although in many cases this may be neither feasible nor practicable

- Interventions should not preclude repeated or other interventions in the future. This concept of 'retreatability' encourages the use of like-for-like repairs, sacrificial repairs and coatings

- All works should be adequately recorded and the records made available to others

1 Cleaning

1.1 Reasons for cleaning

Cleaning is a complex issue as it involves both aesthetic and technical considerations and should be viewed as a major intervention. For this reason, it is important to seek the advice of a qualified conservator or other conservation specialist. Although light cleaning of sound stone with a bristle brush (non-metallic) and clean water is unlikely to cause damage and could be carried out by a volunteer, it is strongly recommended that any other cleaning of a war memorial should only be carried out by experienced craftspeople or conservators.

As a general rule, memorials should be cleaned primarily for technical reasons – for example to remove soiling which is causing damage to the historic material or to allow further treatment to be carried out. The aim of cleaning is not to return the memorial to a 'like new' appearance, but to safely remove particulate deposits, staining and biological growths. A balance has to be struck between accepting the inevitable effects of the passage of time and maintaining a dignified and cared-for appearance. Inscriptions are a more legitimate subject of cleaning, especially if it increases their legibility, although this should not be taken as a licence to clean all areas of a memorial.

Figure 2
Heavy biological growth obscures inscriptions. Careful removal can improve legibility.

Figure 3
Biological growth can grow behind applied lead lettering. Great care must be taken not ot damage or dislodge the lettering when cleaning.

1.2 Cleaning strategy and trials

An appropriate cleaning strategy is one that uses the mildest and least damaging methods to achieve the desired cleaning effect, while minimising any alteration of the underlying material. The method should be controllable (both in practical and health and safety terms) and must not deposit by-products (for example detergents) that cannot be completely removed.

Even quite gentle regular cleaning of stone work can result in increased exposure of the surface pores of the stone; this provides a suitable location for pollutants to collect and biological growth to take root. As a result, the memorial gets dirtier more quickly and a more frequent cycle of cleaning can become established.

An appropriate cleaning strategy requires initial evaluation of:

■ the nature of the material, for example the mineralogy of the stone, the type of metal

■ the condition of the material

■ the nature and extent of soiling

■ the biodiversity and importance of biological growth including lichens, mosses and algae, some of which are protected by law

Initial cleaning trials, carried out in a discreet part of the memorial, are essential, not only to demonstrate the effectiveness of the options but to manage expectations by showing what result cleaning can achieve. The least abrasive and invasive methods should be trialed first before resorting to more aggressive methods. In practice, more than one method may be appropriate for different types of soiling and substrate on different areas of the same memorial.

Figure 4: Trial cleaning areas
Cleaning trials in progress using various poultices to remove deep staining. The trials have been marked out and the poultice applied to complete stones. Assessment should always be carried out several days after the trial has been completed.

1.3 Cleaning methods

Decisions on appropriate cleaning methods are determined on the basis of the considerations above. Table 1 summarises the range of materials to be found on war memorials and a selection of possible cleaning methods.

In all cases, operatives must have experience of using the methods, equipment or chemicals on weathered historic surfaces because inappropriate cleaning can cause irreversible damage. All proprietary methods and materials must be used according to the instructions of the manufacturer or supplier. Some methods may require subsequent rinsing or neutralising.

TABLE 1: Methods of cleaning		Materials											
Cleaning method		Stone					Metal				Timber	Brick	Concrete
		Limestone	Sandstone	Marble	Slate	Granite	Bronze	Brass	Iron	Lead			
Water washing	Brushing with water	●		●	●	●	●	●			●		●
	Mist spraying	●		●	●	●						●	●
	Low pressure washing				●	●			●				●
	Steam	●		●	●	●	●		●	●		●	●
Mechanical	Hand-held	●	●	●	●	●	●	●	●	●	●	●	●
	Dry air-abrasive	●	●	●	●	●			●			●	
	Wet air-abrasive	●	●	●	●	●			●			●	
Chemical	Acid		●			●						●	
	Alkali	●	●		●	●					●		●
	Organic solvents	●	●	●							●		
Poultices		●		●	●	●					●		●
Special	Laser	●	●	●	●	●					●		●

Water washing

Water is an effective solvent and some form of it can be used for cleaning most substrates.

Brushing with water

This is effective at removing water-soluble dirt from many substrates although it is ineffective with sandstone and most types of brick. Brushes should be made from bristle or nylon (not wire) and must not scratch or abrade the surface. Water should be clean and a sponge used to collect any run-off. For bronze and brass a lint-free or microfibre cloth can be used with water; the surface is then wiped off with a dry cloth

Mist spraying

This involves the application of water using anything from hand-held atomised sprays to automated nebulous spray rigs that spray water onto the surface for a short period (usually 5–30 seconds) with a longer interval between (usually 5–10 minutes). The method allows for a minimum of water to be applied and it is particularly useful for dirt that requires softening over a period of time, for example black crusts on limestone, brick and concrete.

Figure 5 (top): War memorial cleaned by hand

Surface biological growth can be removed by scrubbing with water; this is generally less effective than steam, the heat of which helps to kill the root systems of microbiological materials. Also, the act of scrubbing can be damaging if the stone surface is soft or friable.

Figure 6 (bottom): Steam cleaning stone

Steam cleaning in action; the splay of the nozzle and the distance it is held from the stone will depend on the type of stone and the nature of the surface soiling.

Figure 7: Steam-cleaning bronze
High-pressure steam cleaning to remove degraded wax, paint and loose corrosion products, prior to patination.

Low-pressure washing

This is useful for smooth, sound, lightly soiled surfaces such as those of granite, iron and concrete.

For memorials, pressures should normally not exceed 20 bar. Even at these low pressures, the nozzle should be kept at least 20cm from the surface.

It is easy to cause damage with pressure washers (even domestic ones) so they should only be used on a memorial by an experienced operator. They can, however, be used by volunteers to remove slippery algae or organic growth from sound paving slabs.

Steam

Commercial steam cleaners generate a combination of superheated water and steam with a typical temperature of 120–150°C, a flow in the range of 3–10 litres per minute and a nozzle pressure of 30–150 bar. Although this is similar to hot water pressure-washers, the use of an atomising nozzle that diffuses the jet of steam results in a very low pressure at the surface being cleaned. There are also 'dry' steam cleaners that heat the water up to 180°C; these use much less water. Steam is particularly useful for softer organic deposits. Although effective for cleaning around lead lettering, care must be taken that the letters are not dislodged.

Mechanical

Most of the mechanical methods for removing a surface deposit can cause damage if used inappropriately or by inexperienced operators.

Hand-held

These methods include vacuum cleaning, dry brushing, dry sponges and spatulas. The appropriate tool can be used to remove surface dust and debris from most materials. Localised corrosion on bronze can be reduced by careful cleaning with wire wool but this must always be carried out by experienced craftsmen or conservators. A wire brush can be used to remove corrosion products from iron.

Dry air-abrasive

This method can be used for removing thicker or more tenacious dirt, especially if spread over a large area. The equipment consists of a compressor which forces air into a pot containing abrasive particles, and thence through a hose and nozzle. Units work at pressures anywhere between 1.5 and 6.8 bar, and vary from small machines suitable for delicate carved work (micro air abrasion) to more robust industrial units designed for cleaning larger areas. This method of cleaning must always be used by an experienced operator. Nozzle shape, pressure, flow rate, working distance, and the abrasive can all be varied. As a rule, pressures and quantities of abrasive should be kept as low as possible. The method can be used on iron to remove corrosion and paint and locally on bronze to remove green powdery pustules of active corrosion as well as at low pressures on most types of stone. It can, however, cause slight damage to the surface which may lead to accelerated decay or re-soiling. Sandstone is particularly vulnerable to such problems.

Wet air-abrasive

This method combines abrasive cleaning with water cleaning; the addition of water allows more control over the process. Wet air-abrasive systems used in conservation feed the abrasive and the water through separate hoses. A vortex nozzle then allows the aggregate to strike the wall at a shallow angle. This can allow more uniform and less aggressive cleaning. The method is widely used for cleaning black pollution crusts from stone and brick as well as active corrosion products from metals. Unless active corrosion (pitting, pustules and powdering) is present, wet abrasive cleaning methods should not be used on bronze as this will remove evidence of historic patina and can cause surface damage. Where it is used on bronze to remove pitting corrosion, this should be done locally with a suitably sized nozzle.

Figure 8: Wet abrasive cleaning
Pressurised wet abrasive cleaning in action. The water and abrasive are emitted through a vortex nozzle which allows the aggregate to strike the wall at a shallow angle.

Chemical

There is a large range of chemicals that can break down the bonds between dirt or paint and the substrate. Decisions to use chemicals for cleaning will depend on the nature and condition of the substrate and there are many proprietary products to undertake specific cleaning processes.

Chemical cleaners are usually supplied as gels or pastes and manufacturer's instructions must alwaysbe followed. Surfaces should always be well wetted before any chemical is applied, and thoroughly neutralised and rinsed down after wards, perhaps with steam at low pressure. The length of time the chemical is in contact with the stone (which can be reduced by gentle brushing or agitation) andenvironmental conditions are also crucially important.

Acids

These are normally based on low concentrations of a variety of acids. They can be effective for cleaning sandstone and brick (for example brick acid for removing calcite deposits) but can cause salts to form unless they are very well rinsed. The rinsing can introduce lots of water into the substrate, which may itself cause damage (for example leading to the expansion of clays in sandstone).

Alkalis

These are more commonly used and form the basis for many commercial paint strippers. They should not be used on metals but are useful for dissolving black crusts from limestone and for removing applied coatings from timber. Alkali paint strippers are usually supplied in the form of a poultice. They are left in contact for up to 24 hours and prevented from drying out by being covered with polythene.

Organic solvents

These include materials such as acetone and white spirit which are generally used for the localised removal of grease or stains from stone. Other solvents form the basis for non-caustic paint strippers.

Poultices

Poultices are a combination of chemical (including water) and support (such as clay, paper pulp, Fuller's earth or latex). They allow for controlled cleaning by increasing the contact between a chemical and the dirt; this allows for lower concentrations of chemical to be used. However, they must be carefully controlled and optimum contact times established through trials. On war memorials, common poultices might be:

- **Ammonium carbonate.** A solution (around 10% concentration) usually mixed with sepiolite clay and paper pulp and used to dissolve black crusts from limestone.

- **Ammonium chloride and ammonia.** Mixed with paper pulp and Fuller's earth to remove bronze staining from porous stone.

- **Sodium citrate and glycerine.** Applied as a clay poultice to remove iron stains from porous limestones.

- **EDTA (ethylenediamine tetraacetic acid).** Usually applied as a gel or latex poultice to mobilise and remove metallic and other stains from most types of stone. The latex can be synthetic or natural and is normally stabilised with ammonia, which has its own cleaning effect.

Figure 9: Poultice cleaning

An ammonia and clay-based poultice has been used to remove copper sulphate staining. After the poulitce has been applied, drying out is controlled by the application of cling film. Multiple applications may be required.

Figure 10

The poultice has been removed, leaving a cleaned area.

Treatment of biological growth on stone, brick and concrete

There should generally be a presumption against the removal of biological growths; most are harmless. However, they can obscure inscriptions and therefore justify limited cleaning. If assessment shows that treatment is appropriate and necessary, the simplest approach involves physical removal of thicker growths with wooden spatulas, followed by cleaning with water and non-metallic brushes or super-heated steam cleaners.

Growing concern for the environment has made the automatic use of biocides obsolete and untenable. Most modern commercial biocides are aqueous formulations of organo-halogen compounds, quaternary ammonium compounds, metallic salts or oxidising agents.

Only products approved by the Pesticides Safety Directorate (part of the Health and Safety Directorate) may be sold, supplied, stored, advertised or used in the UK. The regulations also cover disposal. Only 'professional' products should be used in public or commercial situations and the application of such biocides must comply with the Conditions of Approval relating to their use. There are additional restrictions placed on the use of biocides in, or near, watercourses. Only certain approved products may be used and the Environment Agency has to authorise such use in each case.

Before even considering biocide use it is important to define what the actual problem is and what options there are for dealing with it –biocides should be the last solution considered. If treatment with biocides is considered the only option, it should be prepared according to the manufacturer's instructions and then carefully applied to the stone surface by trained operatives. It is left in contact with the stone for the recommended dwell time and the treated area covered with polythene. After several days, much of the dead biological growth can be removed through dry brushing with a stiff bristled brush. The process can be repeated and a final application left on the surface to pre vent regrowth. Cleaning may appear incomplete at first, but improvement subsequently occurs as the most tenaciously attached plants, lichens or algae are gradually removed from the stone surface by weathering.

Re-formation of biological growths varies depending on the weather, type of stone, nutrients, pore structure and surface roughness. Some regrowth can be expected after 2–3 years but if there is a significant amount within 6 months, it is likely that the product was unsuitable for the task.

Laser cleaning

This is a comparatively new method of cleaning. The equipment is expensive and requires great expertise. It works by firing pulses of high-energy light, which is absorbed by the dirt and then vaporises; it works best when there is a contrast between dark dirt and a pale substrate. It can be very carefully controlled and is therefore used in situations where the substrate is vulnerable.

Removing graffiti

Graffiti applied to smooth, glazed, impermeable, hard and resistant surfaces can be cleaned relatively easily. Greater problems are encountered with porous rough surfaces such as stone and concrete. The ease of removal will depend on the nature of the medium and the degree of bonding with the substrate.

Graffiti removal involves the dissolution of a wide range of media, including spray paints, marking pens, wax crayons and lipstick. Cleaning is generally done with solvent-based paint strippers in conjunction with super-heated steam cleaners. This is sometimes followed by poultice application of organic solvents to eliminate deeper residues. At all stages, thorough rinsing to remove all traces of chemicals is essential. Removal should be carried out as soon as possible after the graffiti has been applied, since air and sunlight cause some types of graffiti to become considerably more difficult to dissolve. More details are given in the *Historic England Technical Advice Note – Graffiti on Historic Buildings and Monuments: Methods of removal and prevention*.

2 References

2.1 Historic England

Historic England publications are available from HistoricEngland.org.uk/images-books/publications

Caring for Historic Graveyard and Cemetery Monuments
HistoricEngland.org.uk/images-books/publications/caring-historic-graveyard-cemetery-monuments

Conservation Principles, Policies and Guidance
HistoricEngland.org.uk/images-books/publications/conservation-principles-sustainable-management-historic-environment

Designation Listing Selection Guide: Commemorative Structures
HistoricEngland.org.uk/images-books/publications/dlsg-commemorative-structures

Graffiti on Historic Buildings and Monuments: Methods of Removal and Prevention
HistoricEngland.org.uk/images-books/publications/graffiti-on-historic-buildings-and-monuments

Listing War Memorials in England: A Guide for Volunteers
HistoricEngland.org.uk/images-books/publications/listing-war-memorials-in-england/

The Conservation and Management of War Memorial Landscapes
HistoricEngland.org.uk/images-books/publications/conservation-management-war-memorial-landscapes/

The Conservation, Repair and Management of War Memorials
https://HistoricEngland.org.uk/images-books/publications/conservation-repair-management-war-memorials/

The Listing and Grading of War Memorials
HistoricEngland.org.uk/images-books/publications/listing-and-grading-of-war-memorials/

The Setting of Heritage Assets Historic Environment Good Practice in Planning Note 3
HistoricEngland.org.uk/images-books/publications/gpa3-setting-of-heritage-assets/

Types of War Memorial
HistoricEngland.org.uk/images-books/publications/types-of-war-memorial/

Understanding Place: Conservation Area Designation, Appraisal and Management
HistoricEngland.org.uk/images-books/publications/understanding-place-conservation-area

War Memorials Parks and Gardens
HistoricEngland.org.uk/images-books/publications/iha-war-memorial-parks-gardens/

2.2 Practical Building Conservation

This series looks at the conservation of buildings, materials and systems. It builds on the research and field experience of Historic England, and is aimed at those who work on or look after historic buildings.

Practical Building Conservation: Basics (2013)

Practical Building Conservation: Building Environment (2014)

Practical Building Conservation: Concrete (2013)

Practical Building Conservation: Earth, Brick and Terracotta (2015)

Practical Building Conservation: Glass and Glazing (2012)

Practical Building Conservation: Metals (2012)

Practical Building Conservation: Mortars, Renders and Plasters (2012)

Practical Building Conservation: Roofing (2013)

Practical Building Conservation: Stone (2012)

Practical Building Conservation: Timber (2012)

2.3 War Memorials Trust

A complete A–Z of War Memorials Trust helpsheets can be found at: www.warmemorials.org/helpsheets

Condition Survey
www.warmemorials.org/conditionsurvey

Grants and funding
www.warmemorials.org/grants

Ownership of war memorials
www.warmemorials.org/uploads/publications/120.pdf

Preparing a method statement
www.warmemorials.org/uploads/publications/48.pdf

Researching the history of a war memorial
www.warmemorials.org/uploads/publications/122.pdf

Types of contractors and their roles
www.warmemorials.org/uploads/publications/383.pdf

2.4 Other Publications

Ashurst, N 1994 *Cleaning of Historic Buildings*, 2 vols. Shaftesbury: Donhead

Ashurst, J and Dimes, F eds 1990 *Conservation of Building and Decorative Stone.* London: Butterworth-Heinemann

BS 8221-1:2012 *Code of Practice for Cleaning and Surface Repair of Buildings Cleaning of Natural Stone, Brick, Terracotta and Concrete,* London, British Standards Institution

3 Where to Get Advice

3.1 General advice on war memorials

War Memorials Trust
2nd Floor
42a Buckingham Palace Road
London SW1W 0RE

020 7233 7356 or 0300 123 0764
conservation@warmemorials.org
www.warmemorials.org

Historic England
1 Waterhouse Square
138-142 Holborn
London EC1N 2ST

HistoricEngland.org.uk

Details of all listed war memorials can be found at
HistoricEngland.org.uk/listing/the-list/

3.2 Historical research

Commonwealth War Graves Commission
2 Marlow Road
Maidenhead
Berkshire SL6 7DX

01628 634221
www.cwgc.org

Public Monuments and Sculpture Association
70 Cowcross Street
London EC1M 6EJ

020 7490 5001
pmsa@btconnect.com
www.pmsa.org.uk

War Memorials Online
War Memorials Trust
42a Buckingham Palace Road
London SW1W 0RE

020 7233 7356 or 0300 123 0764
www.warmemorialsonline.org.uk

War Memorials Register
c/o Imperial War Museum
Lambeth Road
London SE1 6HZ

020 7207 9851/9863
www.iwm.org.uk/warmemorials

3.3 Conservation Professionals, Specialist Contractors and Conservators

Building Conservation Directory

c/o Cathedral Communications Ltd
High Street
Tisbury
Wiltshire SP3 6HA

01747 871717
info@buildingconservation.com
www.buildingconservation.com

Conservation Register
(for Conservators of Materials)

c/o Institute of Conservation
Unit 1.5 Lafone House
The Leathermarket
Weston Street
London   SE1 3ER

020 3142 6799
conservationregister@icon.org.uk
www.conservationregister.com

Conservation Register
(for Conservation Architects)

c/o Royal Institute of British Architects
66 Portland Place
London   W1B 1AD

020 7580 5533
conservation.register@riba.org
www.architecture.com/conservationregister

Directory of Accredited Conservationists

c/o Chartered Institute of Architectural Technologists
397 City Road
London EC1V 1NH

020 7278 2206
info@ciat.org.uk
www.ciat.org.uk/en/members/conservation-register.
cfm

National Association Of Memorial Masons

1 Castle Mews
Rugby
Warwickshire CV21 2XL

01788 542264
www.namm.org.uk

Register of Accredited
Building Conservation Surveyors

c/o Royal Institution of Chartered Surveyors
Parliament Square
London SW1P 3AD

0870 333 1600
contactrics@rics.org
www.rics.org/uk/join/member-accreditations-list/
building-conservation-accreditation

Register of Architects Accredited
in Building Conservation

AABC Register
No. 5 The Parsonage
Manchester M3 2HS

0161 832 0666
info@aabc-register.co.uk
www.aabc-register.co.uk

3.4 Contact Historic England

East Midlands
2nd Floor, Windsor House
Cliftonville
Northampton NN1 5BE
Tel: 01604 735460
Email: eastmidlands@HistoricEngland.org.uk

East of England
Brooklands
24 Brooklands Avenue
Cambridge CB2 8BU
Tel: 01223 582749
Email: eastofengland@HistoricEngland.org.uk

Fort Cumberland
Fort Cumberland Road
Eastney
Portsmouth PO4 9LD
Tel: 023 9285 6704
Email: fort.cumberland@HistoricEngland.org.uk

London
1 Waterhouse Square
138-142 Holborn
London EC1N 2ST
Tel: 020 7973 3700
Email: london@HistoricEngland.org.uk

North East
Bessie Surtees House
41-44 Sandhill
Newcastle Upon Tyne NE1 3JF
Tel: 0191 269 1255
Email: northeast@HistoricEngland.org.uk

North West
3rd Floor, Canada House
3 Chepstow Street
Manchester M1 5FW
Tel: 0161 242 1416
Email: northwest@HistoricEngland.org.uk

South East
Eastgate Court
195-205 High Street
Guildford GU1 3EH
Tel: 01483 252020
Email: southeast@HistoricEngland.org.uk

South West
29 Queen Square
Bristol BS1 4ND
Tel: 0117 975 1308
Email: southwest@HistoricEngland.org.uk

Swindon
The Engine House
Fire Fly Avenue
Swindon SN2 2EH
Tel: 01793 445050
Email: swindon@HistoricEngland.org.uk

West Midlands
The Axis
10 Holliday Street
Birmingham B1 1TG
Tel: 0121 625 6870
Email: westmidlands@HistoricEngland.org.uk

Yorkshire
37 Tanner Row
York YO1 6WP
Tel: 01904 601948
Email: yorkshire@HistoricEngland.org.uk